Collins Primary Literacy

Pupil Book 1B

Kay Hiatt and Brenda Stones
Series editor: Kay Hiatt

Published by Collins
An imprint of HarperCollins*Publishers*
77–85 Fulham Palace Road
Hammersmith
London
W6 8JB

© HarperCollins*Publishers* Limited 2008

Authors: Kay Hiatt and Brenda Stones
Series editor: Kay Hiatt

10 9 8 7 6 5 4 3 2

ISBN 978 0 00 722694 8

All rights reserved. No part of this publication may be reproduced, stored in a retrieval system, or transmitted in any form or by any means, electronic, mechanical, photocopying, recording or otherwise, without the prior written permission of the Publisher or a licence permitting restricted copying in the United Kingdom issued by the Copyright Licensing Agency Ltd, 90 Tottenham Court Road, London W1T 4LP.

British Library Cataloguing in Publication Data
A Catalogue record for this publication is available from the British Library.

Acknowledgements
The authors and publishers wish to thank the following for permission to use copyright material:
Unit 5: HarperCollins for text and photography from *A Day at the Eden Project* by Kate Petty, text © Kate Petty, 2005 (Collins Big Cat); HarperCollins for photographs from *A Visit to the Farm* by Michael Morpurgo (Collins Big Cat); Unit 6: HarperCollins for text and illustrations from *The Oak Tree* by Anna Owen (Collins Big Cat); Unit 7: "Daddy's Seaside Counting Poem" by Pamela Mordecai, reprinted with kind permission of the author; Egmont Children's Books for text from "One Smiling Grandma" by Anne Marie Linden, text © Anne Marie Linden, 1992 (Heinemann Young Books); Unit 8: Orion Children's Books for illustrations from *The Little Red Hen* from *A Year Full of Stories* by Georgie Adams, 1997 (Orion Children's Books)

Illustrations: Beccy Blake, Julian Mosedale, Shirley Chiang, Gwyneth Williamson, Martin Sanders, Gemma Hastilow

Photographs: p4, top right: Bob Berry; p5, top middle: Bob Berry, top right: Phil Gendall/Eden; p6, middle left: Alamy/imagebroker/Harald Theissen; p12, top: Alamy/Blueberg; p14, top: Rex Features/Dan Thory

Every effort has been made to trace copyright holders and to obtain their permission for the use of copyright material. The authors and publishers will gladly receive any information enabling them to rectify any error or omission in subsequent editions.

Browse the complete Collins catalogue at
www.collinseducation.com

Printed in Hong Kong by Printing Express Ltd

Mixed Sources
Product group from well-managed forests and other controlled sources
www.fsc.org Cert no. SW-COC-1806
© 1996 Forest Stewardship Council

FSC is a non-profit international organisation established to promote the responsible management of the world's forests. Products carrying the FSC label are independently certified to assure consumers that they come from forests that are managed to meet the social, economic and ecological needs of present and future generations.

Find out more about HarperCollins and the environment at
www.harpercollins.co.uk/green

Contents

Page number

Unit 5	Our Day Out	4
Unit 6	Finding Out	12
Unit 7	Counting Poems	22
Unit 8	Tell Me a Story	34

5 Our Day Out

This unit helps you read, talk and write about what you've done during the day.

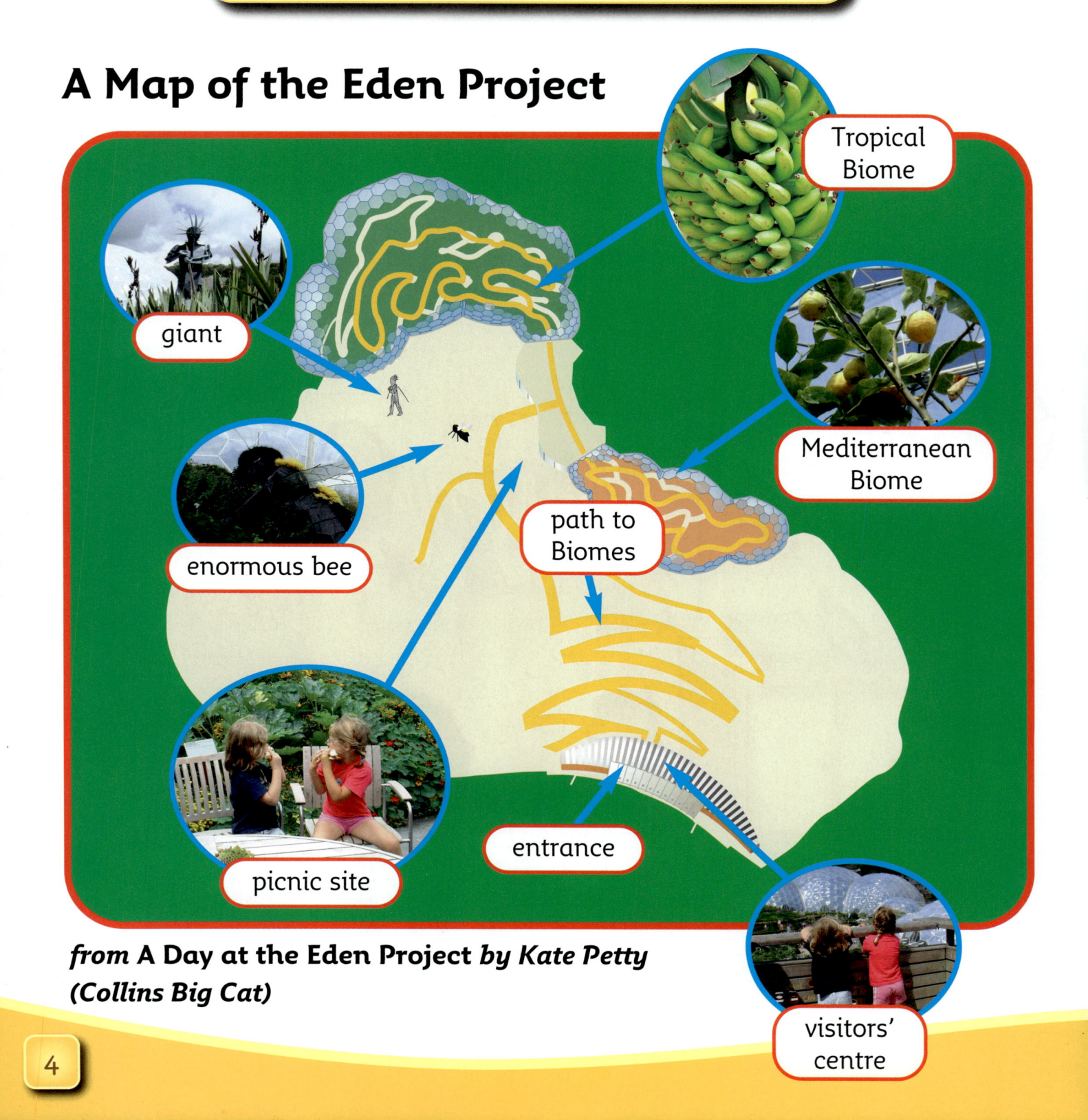

A Map of the Eden Project

- Tropical Biome
- giant
- Mediterranean Biome
- enormous bee
- path to Biomes
- picnic site
- entrance
- visitors' centre

from **A Day at the Eden Project** *by Kate Petty* **(Collins Big Cat)**

Unit 5 Our Day Out

1 Talk/pair/share

Look at these pictures.
Talk about what you think these are.

| a pineapple | a bunch of bananas | cocoa pods |

2 Speaking and listening

Work in pairs. You're going to visit the Eden Project. What would you like to see?

Talk about your visit.

First …

Next …

Then …

After …

Finally …

5

A Visit to the Farm

Unit 5 Our Day Out

3 Write/pair/share

Work in pairs.
Write some sentences about each animal.

Geese are large birds.
They can hiss.

4 Reading and thinking

Look at the pictures. Answer these questions.

1. Look at the top two pictures. Why is the cow bigger than the calf?
2. Why is the lamb smaller than the sheep?
3. A baby horse is called a foal. Find a picture of a foal and copy it.
4. Baby hens are called chicks. Find a picture of a chick and copy it.
5. Baby geese are called goslings. Find a picture of a gosling and copy it.

7

A Visit to Scary Farm

Welcome to Scary Farm.

Here are the animals at Scary Farm.

lion

shark

monster

snake

crocodile

spider

Unit 5 Our Day Out

5 Think/pair/share

Make a timetable for your day at Scary Farm.
Here are some ideas.

Muck out the lions.

Count the spiders.

Exercise the crocodiles.

Feed the sharks.

Collect the snakes' eggs.

Drive the monsters out onto the fields.

Set it out like this.

	Our timetable
7:30am	Drive the monsters out onto the fields.
8:30am	BREAKFAST
9:30am	
11:00am	
12:30pm	LUNCH
1:45pm	
3:45pm	
5:00pm	HOME

6 Drawing a postcard

Make a postcard from Scary Farm.
Draw the picture for the front of the card.

Unit 5 Our Day Out

7 Writing a postcard

Write a postcard to your friend. Tell them what you did at Scary Farm.

Plan what you say on the postcard.

Dear ...

We had a great time at Scary Farm.

First we ...

Then we ...

Finally we ...

Remember!
- Write in full sentences.
- Start with a capital letter.
- End with a full stop.

What I have learned
- I can write lists and sentences.
- I can talk about planning a visit.
- I can write what I did on a day out.

11

6 Finding Out

This unit helps you find out facts and use them in your writing.

The Oak Tree

This is an oak tree.

- trunk
- leaves
- branches
- bark
- roots

Unit 6 Finding Out

1 Talk/pair/share

Plan some questions about the oak tree.
You can use these words to start your questions.

What? **Who?** **Why?**

How? **Where?** **When?**

How does the tree stand up?

2 Write/pair/share

Write the questions.
Choose your best question.
Ask your teacher your question.

What lives in the branches?

13

This is the trunk.

Who lives in the trunk?

owls

woodpeckers

Unit 6 Finding Out

3 Talk/pair/share

Look at the pictures and the words on pages 14, 16 and 17.

Tell your partner what you can find out.

The baby woodpeckers are in a nest.

Different kinds of birds live in an oak tree.

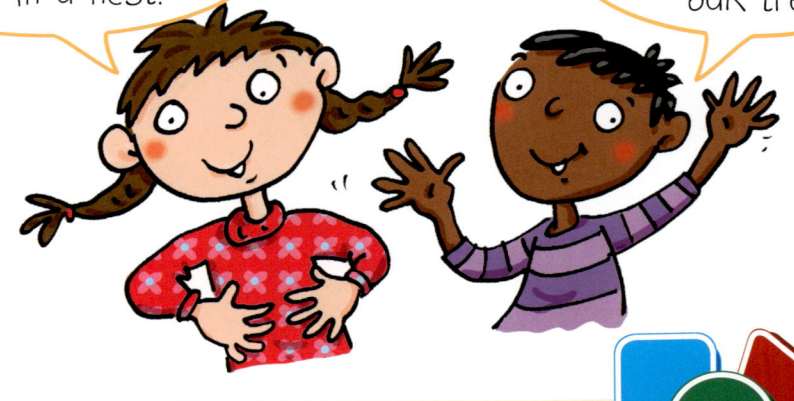

4 Writing facts

Write at least one sentence about what you've found out.

Start with a capital letter and end with a full stop.

Woodpeckers live in the trunk.

15

butterfly

squirrel

fox

5 Alphabetical order

Look at the picture of the oak tree on this page. Read the words on the labels. Put the words in alphabetical order.

ant

bat

Unit 6 Finding Out

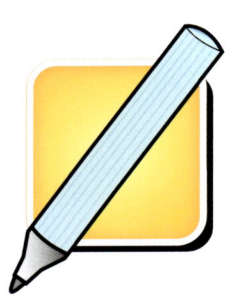

crow
bat
caterpillar
owl
beetle
woodpecker
wasp
ant
worm
mole
rabbit

from **The Oak Tree** *by Anna Owen (Collins Big Cat)*

6 Making a glossary

Work with a partner. Use your list of words from Activity 5. Write what the words mean.

ant a tiny insect with six legs

bat an animal with wings that hangs upside down

All About Ants

Ants have six legs and a body in four parts.

body   head

legs

They are tiny creatures that work very hard.

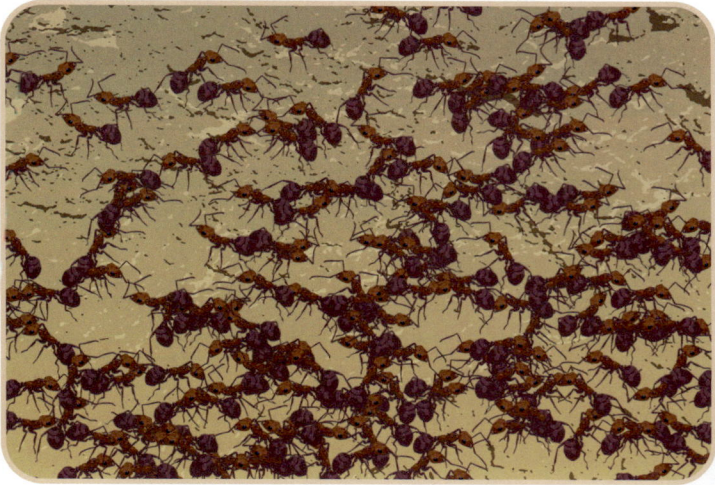

They live in large groups called colonies.

Their homes are nests in the ground, or under bricks or old wood.

They gather leaves for their food.

Unit 6 Finding Out

They lay eggs which hatch into baby ants.

Ants are really amazing. They can pass messages to each other. They can learn from each other.

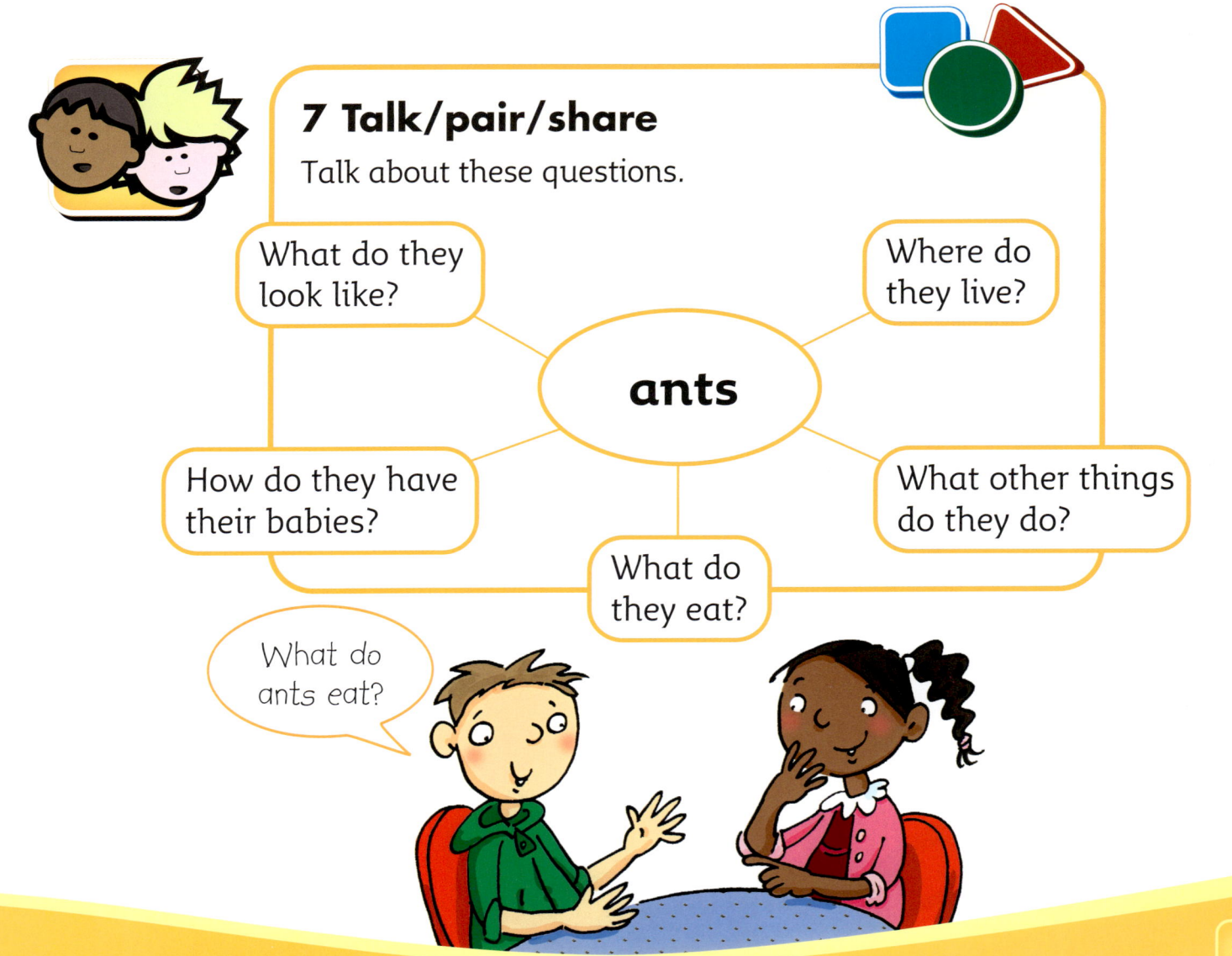

7 Talk/pair/share

Talk about these questions.

- What do they look like?
- Where do they live?
- How do they have their babies?
- What other things do they do?
- What do they eat?

ants

What do ants eat?

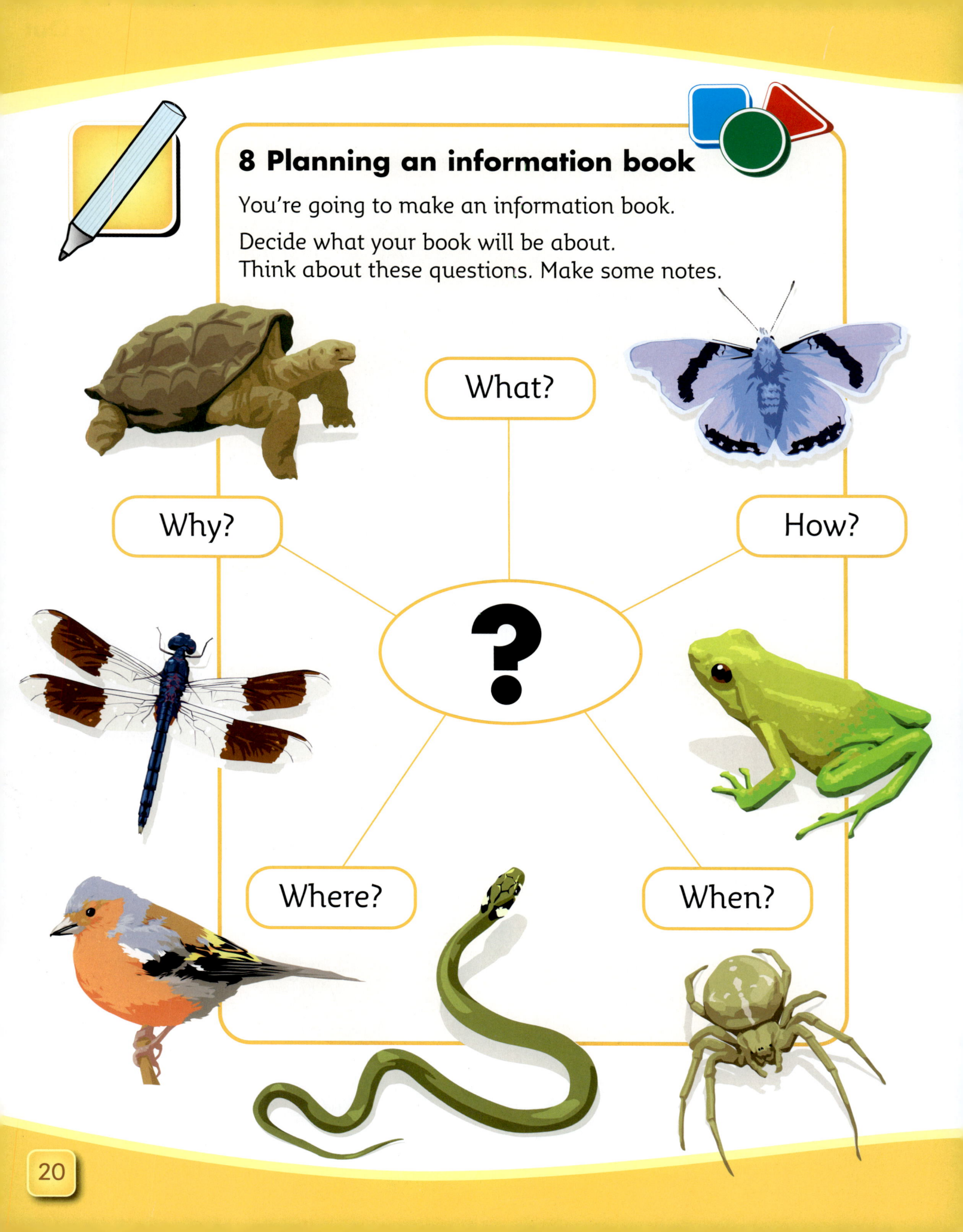

8 Planning an information book

You're going to make an information book.

Decide what your book will be about.
Think about these questions. Make some notes.

- What?
- Why?
- How?
- Where?
- When?

Unit 6 Finding Out

9 Writing an information book

Use your notes to make the pages.

Glossary

Contents

Owls

Remember!

Your book could include:

- a cover
- a contents list
- pictures and labels
- captions
- a glossary.

What I have learned

- I can find out information.
- I can read labels and text.
- I can write my own information.

21

7 Counting Poems

This unit helps you learn about rhythm and rhyme in poems. You'll write your own poem at the end.

Ten Little Fingers

I have ten little fingers,
And they all belong to me.
I can make them do things.
Would you like to see?

Unit 7 Counting Poems

I can shut them
up tight,

Or open them
all wide.

I can put them
all together,

Or make them
all hide.

23

I can make them
jump high,

I can make
them jump low,

I can fold
them quietly,
And sit just so.

Unit 7 Counting Poems

1 Reading the poem aloud

1. Practise the actions.

2. Find the rhyming words.

   Write them in a list like this. The first one is done for you.

   me – see
   wide – ___
   low – ___

Daddy's Seaside Counting Poem

One baby starfish
smaller than my hand

Two bright fishing boats
lying on the sand

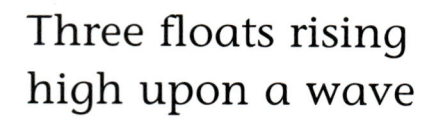

Three floats rising
high upon a wave

Four boys catching crabs
in a dark cave

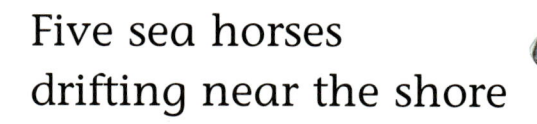

Five sea horses
drifting near the shore

Unit 7 Counting Poems

Six fat jellyfish –
maybe there are more!

Seven ripe coconuts
with sweet white meat

Eight buried bodies …
how many feet?

Nine seagulls flying
far out at sea

Ten hungry children
looking up at me.

Pamela Mordecai

2 Performing the poem

Work in a group. Decide what actions you want to do for each part of the poem.

Practise your actions.

Perform your poem and actions for another group.

3 Thinking and telling

Practise saying what you liked about the way the group performed the poem.

Think about these questions:

Which actions did you like best?

What would you change?

Unit 7 Counting Poems

4 Reading and understanding

Read the poem again.
Talk about these questions for ■ , ● or ▲ .

■
1. How big is the starfish?
2. Where are the boys?
3. What is inside the coconuts?

▲
1. Which **two** words tell you the starfish is little?
2. Why do you think the crabs are in a dark cave?
3. How many bodies are buried?

●
1. How big is the starfish?
2. Where are the three floats?
3. What are the seagulls looking for? Look at the picture!

5 Drawing new pictures

Now draw pictures for these new lines:

Eleven sparkly seashells shining in the sun

Twelve happy children having lots of fun.

29

One Smiling Grandma

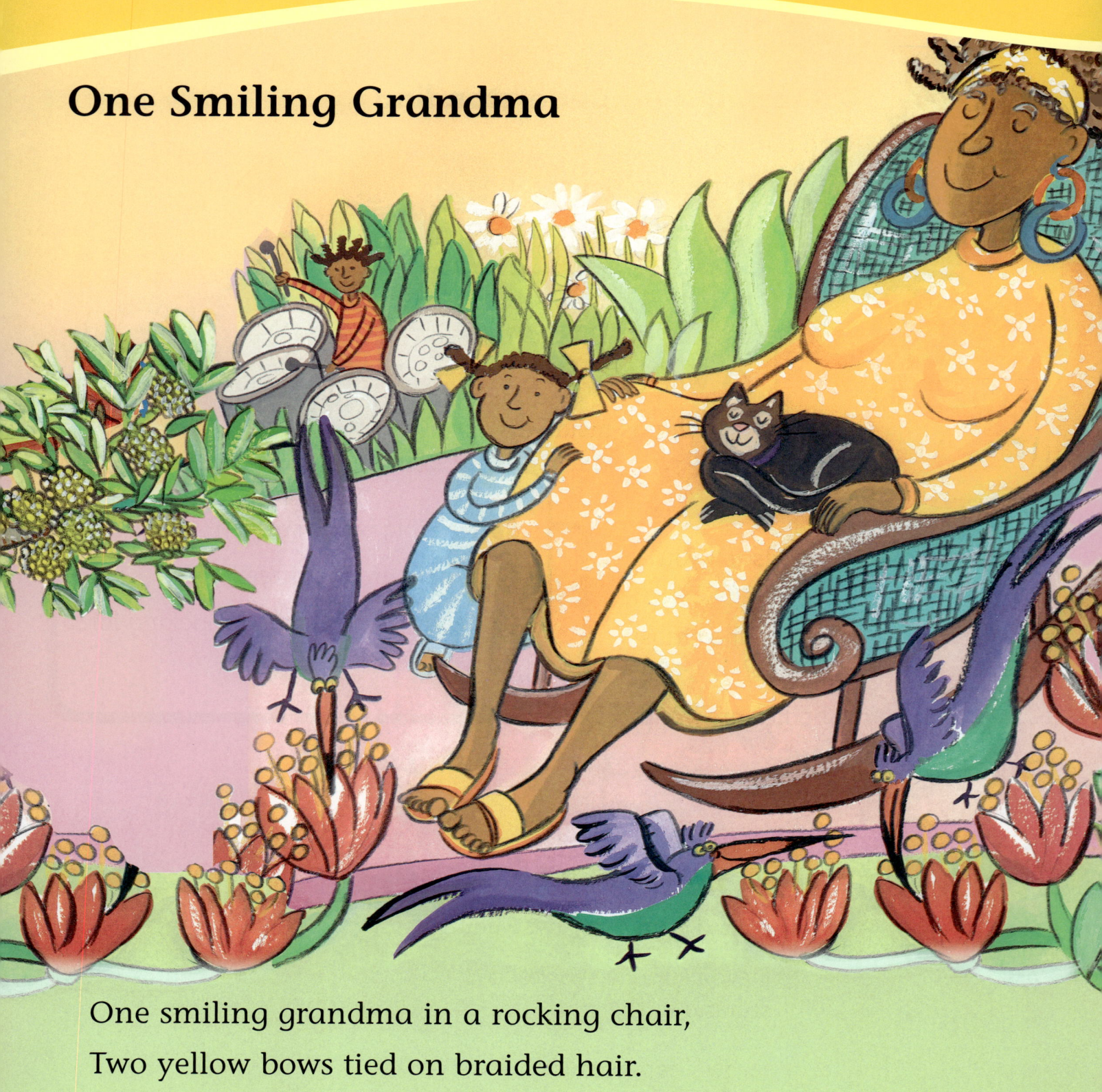

One smiling grandma in a rocking chair,
Two yellow bows tied on braided hair.
Three hummingbirds sipping nectar sweet,
Four steel drums tapping out the beat.

Unit 7 Counting Poems

Five flying fish gliding through the air,
Six market ladies selling their wares.
Seven conch shells I find on the beach,
Eight sugar apples, just out of reach.
Nine hairy coconuts, hard and round,
Ten sleepy mongooses. Hush! Not a sound.

Anne Marie Linden

6 Using your senses

Listen to the poem with your eyes closed.
Think about these questions:

What can I hear?

What can I touch?

What can I see?

What can I taste?

What can I smell?

Unit 7 Counting Poems

7 Writing a poem

Add your own words to the poem.

You can use ideas from the picture to help you.

One _____ _____ in a rocking chair,
Two _____ _____ tied on braided hair.
Three _____ _____ sipping nectar sweet,
Four _____ _____ tapping out the beat.
Five _____ _____ gliding through the air,

Six _____ _____ selling their wares.
Seven _____ _____ I find on the beach,
Eight _____ _____, just out of reach.
Nine _____ _____, hard and round,
Ten _____ _____. Hush! Not a sound.

What I have learned

- I can read poems aloud.
- I know that poems have words that rhyme.
- I can write simple poems.

8 Tell Me a Story

This unit is about telling stories that have pattern and shape to them.

The Gingerbread Man

1.

2. Run! Run! As fast as you can! You can't catch me, I'm the Gingerbread Man!

3.

4.

Unit 8 Tell Me a Story

from The Gingerbread Man *retold by Karina Law*

1 Drama

Work in a group. Perform the story of *The Gingerbread Man*.

Think of a new ending.

"What a yummy little gingerbread man!"

"I'd like to munch you! I'd like to crunch you!"

"You can't catch me, I'm the Gingerbread Man!"

Unit 8 Tell Me a Story

2 Write/pair/share

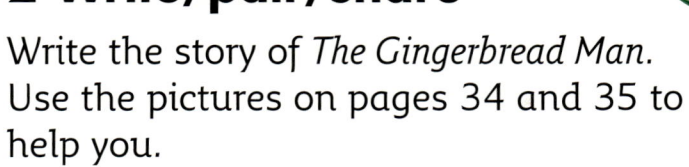

Write the story of *The Gingerbread Man*. Use the pictures on pages 34 and 35 to help you.

Draw a picture for your new ending.

37

3 Sitting in the hot seat

Think of questions to ask these characters in the story.

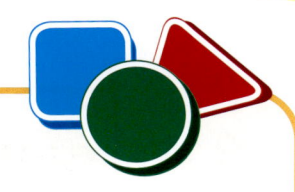

1. the old woman 
2. the cow 
3. the horse 
4. the fox 
5. the gingerbread man

How did you feel?

Did you like the gingerbread man?

Why did you run away?

38

Unit 8 Tell Me a Story

4 Role play

Pretend you are the fox. Are you a good fox or a bad fox?

Think of reasons why you **should** eat the gingerbread man.

Then think of reasons why you **shouldn't** eat the gingerbread man.

I should eat the gingerbread man because …

I shouldn't eat the gingerbread man because …

5 Talk/pair/share

Talk about this story table with your partner.

Characters – Who was in the story?

Beginning – What happened at the beginning?

Middle – What happened in the middle?

Ending – What happened at the end?

Unit 8 Tell Me a Story

6 Think/pair/share

Think about other stories and rhymes you know.

Choose one and fill in a story table for it.

Characters Who was in the story?	
Beginning What happened at the beginning?	
Middle What happened in the middle?	
Ending What happened at the end?	

The Little Red Hen

1

2

3

Unit 8 Tell Me a Story

4

5

What does this story teach us?

from The Little Red Hen by Georgie Adams

7 Talk/pair/share

Work in pairs. Talk about this story table for *The Little Red Hen*.

Characters – Who was in the story?

Beginning – What happened at the beginning?

Middle – What happened in the middle?

Ending – What happened at the end?

Unit 8 Tell Me a Story

8 Think/pair/share

Work in pairs. Pretend you are the cat and the dog. Think about these questions:

- Why should you be lazy?
- Why should you be helpful?

We should be lazy because …

We shouldn't be lazy because …

9 Reading and responding

Talk about these questions:

1. Why did Little Red Hen work so hard?

2. Did Little Red Hen like cat and dog?

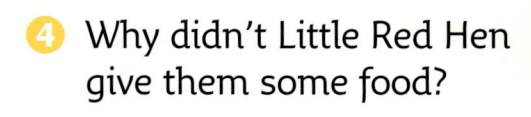

3. Why were cat and dog so lazy?

4. Why didn't Little Red Hen give them some food?

10 Role play

You're going to interview Little Red Hen. Think what questions you'd like to ask.

Do you like working hard?

Why do you think cat and dog are lazy?

Unit 8 Tell Me a Story

11 Planning a story

You're going to plan your own story about a lazy horse and a clever farmer.

> The farmer needs to get his potatoes to market.
> The lazy horse doesn't want to go.
> How will the farmer make his horse go?

Talk to your partner and decide on your story.
Make a story table.

Draw a storyboard and write captions.

12 Writing a story

Write your story using your story plans from Activity 11.

Here are some useful words:

Once upon a time ...

The clever farmer said ...

The lazy horse said ...

First the farmer ...

Next the farmer ...

At last ...

What I have learned

- I know that every story has characters and a beginning, middle and ending.
- I can plan the parts of a story.
- I can write a story.

48